A Paines Plc

C000212161

Growth

by Luke Norris

Growth was first commissioned and performed by the
Royal Welsh College of Music and Drama in collaboration
with Paines Plough in April 2015, directed by Sean Linnen.

The play opened on 6 August 2016 in Paines Plough's
Roundabout @ Summerhall, Edinburgh Festival Fringe,
in a new production by Paines Plough.

Supported by
**ARTS COUNCIL
ENGLAND**

Growth

by Luke Norris

Cast

Remy Beasley
Richard Corgan
Andy Rush

Creative Team

Direction	George Perrin
Lighting Design	Prema Mehta
Sound Design/Composition	Dominic Kennedy
Assistant Director	Anna Himali Howard
Senior Producer	Hanna Streeter
Producer	Francesca Moody
Assistant Producer	Sofia Stephanou
Company Stage Manager	Caitlin O'Reilly
Technical Stage Managers	Callum Thomson
	Hamish Ellis
Programmer	Peter Small
Movement Consultant	Kate Sagovsky
Costume Supervisor	Kat Smith

LUKE NORRIS (Writer)

Luke's latest play, *So Here We Are*, debuted at the HighTide Festival in September 2015 before transferring to Manchester Royal Exchange. It won a Bruntwood Judges' Award and was nominated for two Manchester Theatre Awards.

His professional debut *Goodbye To All That* was performed at the Jerwood Theatre Upstairs at the Royal Court, London, and was widely acclaimed; the *Telegraph* commented that 'we're in the presence, unquestionably, of a playwright of major promise'. His next performed work was *Hearts* for NT Connections, which played at the Sheffield Crucible and The Shed at the National Theatre.

In 2014 Luke was commissioned to write a play by the Royal Welsh College of Music and Drama and Paines Plough, out of which came *Growth*. It was performed in Cardiff in March before transferring to the Gate, London, in April 2015.

He is currently under commission to the Bush Theatre, London, and is writing a new radio play for BBC Radio 4.

REMY BEASLEY

Remy trained at Royal Welsh College of Music and Drama.

Theatre credits include: *The Insatiable, Inflatable Candylion, Love Steals Us From Loneliness, Silly Kings* (National Theatre Wales); *Symphony* (nabokov/Vault Festival/ Lyric Hammersmith/National Theatre Live); *The Taming of the Shrew* (Shakespeare's Globe); *Little Dogs* (Frantic Assembly/ National Theatre Wales); *Nabokov Fairytales, It's About Time* (nabokov); *Gaslight* (Clwyd Theatr Cymru).

Television credits include: *Gwaith Cartref* (Fiction Factory); *Stella* (Tidy Productions/ Sky One); *Critical* (Sky One); *Perfect Summer* (BBC Wales Television).

Film credits include: *Love is Thicker Than Water* (Mulholland Pictures + Barnsbury Pictures).

RICHARD CORGAN

Richard trained at Bristol Old Vic Theatre School.

Theatre credits include: *Tom: A Story of Tom Jones – The Musical* (No:1 UK tour); *Macbeth, The Changeling* (Barbican/ Tobacco Factory); *Press OK R&D* (National Theatre); *The Merchant of Venice* (Singapore Repertory Theatre); *Gardening: For the Unfulfilled and Alienated* (Latitude Festival/Edinburgh Fringe, Fringe First winner); *A Provincial Life* (National Theatre Wales); *The Taming of the Shrew, Macbeth, Twelfth Night* (Sprite Productions); *The Taming of the Shrew* (Shakespeare's Globe); *Romeo and Juliet* (LCM); *Flowers From Tunisia* (Torch); *Boeing Boeing* (RCT); *Frozen, Merlin and the Cave of Dreams* (Sherman Cymru); *Othello, Cyrano de Bergerac* (Royal Opera House); *The Long and the Short and the Tall* (Pleasance, Islington); *White Devil* (Redgrave); *NSFW* (Waking Exploits).

Television credits include: *Baker Boys, The B-Word* (BBC Wales); series regular in *Doctors, Caught in the Web* (BBC); *Pobol Y Cwm* (S4C); *Her Majesty The Queen's 80th Birthday Party at the Palace* (BBC Live).

Film credits include: *Canaries* (Maple Dragon); *Diana* (Ecosse Films); *Magpie* (Nowhere Fast Productions).

Radio credits include: *Foursome* (BBC Radio 4); *Blue Remembered Hills* (Christchurch Studios); *Great Ormond St Christmas Carol* (LBC).

ANDY RUSH

Andy trained at Birmingham School of Acting.

Theatre credits include: *Tipping the Velvet* (Lyric Hammersmith); *Unidentified Item in the Bagging Area* (Pink Snail Theatre Company); *Jumpers for Goalposts* (Paines Plough); *A Midsummer Night's Dream, Love's Labour's Lost* (The Lamb Players); *Hello/Goodbye* (Hampstead); *The Kitchen Sink* (Bush); *Sense* (Made By Brick); *Anna Karenina* (Arcola); *Romeo and Juliet* (Cheltenham Everyman).

Television credits include: *Waterloo Road* (Headstrong Pictures); *Tommy Cooper – Not Like That, Like This* (Left Bank Pictures); *Wizards vs Aliens* (BBC); *New Tricks* (Wall to Wall).

Film credits include: *Id2: Shadwell Army* (Parrallax Pictures); *Here & Now* (Small But Tall Films Ltd).

GEORGE PERRIN (Direction)

George is joint Artistic Director of Paines Plough and was formerly joint Artistic Director of nabokov. Directing credits for Paines Plough include: *Love, Lies and Taxidermy* by Alan Harris, *Growth* by Luke Norris, *I Got Superpowers For My Birthday* by Katie Douglas (Roundabout season 2016, Edinburgh Festival Fringe and national tour), *Every Brilliant Thing* by Duncan Macmillan with Jonny Donahoe (national and international tour/Barrow

Street Theater, New York), *The Silver Drills* by Robin French (BBC Radio 4), *Lungs* by Duncan Macmillan, *The Human Ear* and *The Initiate* by Alexandra Wood, *Our Teacher's a Troll* by Dennis Kelly (Roundabout season 2014/15, Edinburgh Festival Fringe/national tour), *Not the Worst Place* by Sam Burns (Sherman Cymru/Theatr Clwyd); *Sea Wall* by Simon Stephens (Dublin Theatre Festival/National Theatre Shed); *Good With People* by David Harrower (59East59 Theatres New York/Traverse/Òran Mór), *London* by Simon Stephens (national tour), *Sixty Five Miles* by Matt Hartley (Hull Truck), *The 8th* by Che Walker and Paul Heaton (Latitude Festival/Barbican/Manchester International Festival/national tour), *DIG* by Katie Douglas (Òran Mór/national tour) and *Juicy Fruits* by Leo Butler (Òran Mór/national tour).

As Trainee Associate Director of Paines Plough, directing credits include: *House of Agnes* by Levi David Addai, *The Dirt Under the Carpet* by Rona Munro, *Crazy Love* by Che Walker, *My Little Heart Dropped in Coffee* by Duncan Macmillan and *Babies* by Katie Douglas.

Directing credits for nabokov include: *2nd May 1997* by Jack Thorne (Bush); *Terre Haute* by Edmund White (59East59 Theatres New York/West End/national tour/Assembly Rooms, Edinburgh Festival Fringe); *Is Everyone OK?* and *Public Displays of Affection* by Joel Horwood and *Camarilla* by Van Badham (nabokov).

PREMA MEHTA (Lighting Design)
Prema graduated from the Guildhall School of Music and Drama.

She has designed the lighting for over one hundred drama and dance productions and installations across the UK including: *Maaya* (Westminster Hall); *Bells* (Mayor of London's outdoor festival, Showtime); *Wipers* (Leicester Curve/UK tour); *Coming Up, Jefferson's Garden* (Watford Palace Theatre); *With a Little Bit of Luck* (Latitude Festival/UK tour); *The Dishonoured*, nominated for The Offies Best New Play (Arcola/UK tour); *The Massacre* (Theatre Royal, Bury St. Edmunds); *Hercules* by New Art Club (Nottingham Playhouse/UK tour); *Red Snapper* (Belgrade, Coventry); *The Great Extension* (Theatre Royal Stratford East); *Snow Queen* (Derby); *The Electric Hills* (Liverpool Everyman); *Sufi Zen* (Royal Festival Hall); *Dhamaka* (O2 Arena).

Prema's design work for the A-List party area at Madame Tussauds in London is open to the public throughout the year.

Current and forthcoming lighting designs include *Lady Anna: All At Sea*, directed by Colin Blumenau and *Spring Awakening*, directed by Nikolai Foster.

Full credits and production gallery can be viewed at www.premamehta.com

DOMINIC KENNEDY (Sound Design)
Dominic is a Sound Designer and Music Producer for performance and live events, he has a keen interest in developing new work and implementing sound and music at an early stage in a creative process. Dominic is a graduate from Royal Central School of Speech and Drama where he developed specialist skills in collaborative and devised theatre making, music composition and installation practices. His work often fuses found sound, field recordings, music composition and synthesis. Dominic has recently designed for and collaborated with Paines Plough, Goat and Monkey, Jamie Wood, Gameshow, Manchester Royal Exchange, Engineer, Outbox, Jemima James and Mars Tarrab. Recent installation work includes interactive sound design for Gingerline (pop-up restaurant pioneers) and the launch of Terry Pratchett's *The Shepherd's Crown*.

Recent theatre credits include: *With a Little Bit of Luck* (nationwide tour); *The Human Ear*, *Our Teacher's a Troll* (Roundabout); *The Devil Speaks True* (The Vaults/nationwide tour); *Run* (New Diorama); *ONO* (Soho); *Crocodiles* (Manchester Royal Exchange); *Karagular* (Shoreditch Town Hall).

ANNA HIMALI HOWARD (Assistant Director)
Anna is a theatremaker and director who graduated from the University of Warwick in 2015. Prior to joining Paines Plough, Anna was a performer and deviser in Breach Theatre's *The Beanfield,* which received a Total Theatre Award at the Edinburgh Fringe in 2015 and toured nationally in 2016. She is a Creative Associate at the Gate Theatre, where she assistant directed *In the Night Time (Before the Sun Rises)* by Nina Segal, and an alumnus of the REP Foundry artist development scheme. Other credits include *Life is No Laughing Matter* by Demi Nandhra as director (Battersea Arts Centre, Normal? Festival) and *20B* by Jane English as dramaturg (Birmingham REP, Theatre Royal Stratford East).

Paines Plough

Paines Plough is the UK's national theatre of new plays. We commission and produce the best playwrights and tour their plays far and wide. Whether you're in Liverpool or Lyme Regis, Scarborough or Southampton, a Paines Plough show is coming to a theatre near you soon.

'The lifeblood of the UK's theatre ecosystem' *Guardian*

Paines Plough was formed in 1974 over a pint of Paines bitter in The Plough pub. Since then we've produced more than 130 new productions by world renowned playwrights like Stephen Jeffreys, Abi Morgan, Sarah Kane, Mark Ravenhill, Dennis Kelly and Mike Bartlett. We've toured those plays to hundreds of places from Manchester to Moscow to Maidenhead.

'That noble company Paines Plough, de facto national theatre of new writing' *Telegraph*

Our Programme 2015 saw 12 productions by the nation's finest writers touring to 84 places from Cornwall to the Orkney Islands; in village halls and Off-Broadway, at music festivals and student unions, online and on radio, and in our own pop-up theatre Roundabout.

With Programme 2016 we continue to tour the length and breadth of the UK from clubs and pubs to lakeside escapes and housing estates. Roundabout hosts our most ambitious Edinburgh Festival Fringe programme ever and brings mini-festivals to each stop on its autumn tour. We're extending our digital reach by live streaming shows and launching our free Come To Where I'm From app featuring over 100 audio plays.

'I think some theatre just saved my life' @kate_clement on Twitter

ROUNDABOUT

'A beautifully designed masterpiece in engineering... a significant breakthrough in theatre technology.' *The Stage*

Roundabout is Paines Plough's beautiful portable in-the-round theatre. It's a completely self-contained 168-seat auditorium that flat packs into a lorry and pops up anywhere from theatres to school halls, sports centres, warehouses, car parks and fields.

We built Roundabout to enable us to tour to places that don't have theatres. For the next decade Roundabout will travel the length and breadth of the UK bringing the nation's best playwrights and a thrilling theatrical experience to audiences everywhere.

In 2015 alone, Roundabout played host to 380 hours of activity, including more than 200 performances by Paines Plough. Over 25,000 people saw a show in Roundabout.

Roundabout was designed by Lucy Osborne and Emma Chapman at Studio Three Sixty in collaboration with Charcoalblue and Howard Eaton.

WINNER of Theatre Building of the Year at The Stage Awards 2014

'Roundabout venue wins most beautiful interior venue by far @edfringe.'
@ChaoticKirsty on Twitter

'Roundabout is a beautiful, magical space. Hidden tech make it Turkish-bath-tranquil but with circus-tent-cheek. Aces.'
@evenicol on Twitter

Roundabout was made possible thanks to the belief and generous support of the following Trusts and individuals and all who named a seat in Roundabout. We thank them all.

TRUSTS AND FOUNDATIONS
Andrew Lloyd Webber Foundation
Paul Hamlyn Foundation
Garfield Weston Foundation
J Paul Getty Jnr Charitable Trust
John Ellerman Foundation

CORPORATE
Universal Consolidated Group
Howard Eaton Lighting Ltd
Charcoalblue
Avolites Ltd
Factory Settings
Total Solutions

Pop your name on a seat and help us pop-up around the UK:
www.justgiving.com/fundraising/roundaboutauditorium

www.painesplough.com/roundabout
#roundaboutpp

Paines Plough

Joint Artistic Directors	James Grieve
	George Perrin
Senior Producer	Hanna Streeter
General Manager	Aysha Powell
Producer	Francesca Moody
Assistant Producer	Sofia Stephanou
Administrator	Simone Ibbett-Brown
Marketing and Audience	Jack Heaton
Development Officer	
Production Assistant	Harriet Bolwell
Finance and Admin Assistant	Charlotte Walton
Technical Director	Colin Everitt
Trainee Director	Anna Himali Howard
Big Room Playwright Fellow	Sam Steiner
Press Representative	The Corner Shop
Designer	Thread Design Studio
	Michael Windsor-Ungureanu

Board of Directors

Caro Newling (Chair), Christopher Bath, Tamara Cizeika, Kim Grant, Nia Janis, Dennis Kelly, Matthew Littleford, Anne McMeehan, Christopher Millard, Cindy Polemis, and Andrea Stark.

Paines Plough Limited is a company limited by guarantee and a registered charity.
Registered Company no: 1165130
Registered Charity no: 267523

Paines Plough, 4th Floor, 43 Aldwych, London WC2B 4DN
+ 44 (0) 20 7240 4533
office@painesplough.com
www.painesplough.com

 Follow @PainesPlough on Twitter

 Like Paines Plough at facebook.com/PainesPloughHQ

 Follow @painesplough on Instagram

Donate to Paines Plough at justgiving.com/PainesPlough

Supported by
ARTS COUNCIL ENGLAND

GROWTH

Luke Norris

'Growth is the only evidence of life'
John Henry Newman

Acknowledgements

Thanks to all at Paines Plough and RWCMD for giving me the opportunity to write a new play in the first place, and to the original RWCMD cast – Ellie Heydon, Jonny Holden, Oliver Morgan-Thomas, Nina Shenkman, Melanie Stevens and Sam Ward – for the commitment and skill brought to bear on the play's first incarnation.

Special thanks go to Sean Linnen for directing that version with such sensitivity and conviction. I owe you one.

Thanks to Andy, Remy and Richard, George, Anna, and Caitlin for the relentless energy and goodwill showered on this version, and for putting up with the endless script changes.

A particularly huge thank-you to Simon Bubb for the unwavering generosity and frankness in helping me research the play.

And finally, as ever, thanks to Jo, for all the hours of enforced dramaturgy...

I promise I'll split the money this time.

L.N.

Characters

TOBES
BETH
JARED
ELLIE
JOFF
LILY
JULIAN
LISE
JUSTIN
BESS
JACK
BILLIE
JERMAINE
LIZA
JAMIE
IZZY
JOEL

A Note on the Punctuation

Generally speaking, speeches should come quickly one after the next. To indicate and encourage this, many lines are written without a full stop at the end

Full stops, meanwhile, don't necessarily mean the end of a thought. Sometimes they do. But. Sometimes they just indicate a hiatus.

Forward slashes (/) within speeches indicate the point at which the next character starts speaking.

An ellipsis (…) in place of a speech indicates a pressure or an attempt to speak.

Beats are of varying length, relative to the pace of the scene. Long beats are longer. Obviously.

A question without a question mark indicates a flatness of tone.

I think that's it.

It's probably not.

This text went to press before the end of rehearsals and so may differ slightly from the play as performed.

One

BETH*'s flat.*

TOBES *and* BETH.

TOBES. What?

BETH. I don't

TOBES....

BETH. Don't make me say it again

TOBES. No, do. Do say it again. So I know you mean it

BETH. I don't, Tobes

TOBES. Why?

BETH....

TOBES. Why not?

BETH. I just. I'm sorry, I don't. Not like I should

TOBES. But why?

BETH. There's not *one* reason

TOBES. Then give me a few. Give me ten. Or twenty. Give me something, Beth

BETH. It's not about you, Tobes

TOBES. No?

BETH. No, not really, / no

TOBES. Because it feels like it might be

BETH. It's not

TOBES. Who's it about then?

BETH. Me. I suppose

TOBES. You suppose?

BETH. Yeah, mainly

TOBES. What does that mean?

BETH....

TOBES. I mean there's no one else is there?

BETH. No

TOBES. Like. That, from your gym, / that

BETH. No! No

TOBES. You'd tell me?

BETH. Yes

TOBES. You would tell me?

BETH. I am telling you

TOBES. It's not him, then? That meat-head?

BETH. Who?

TOBES. 'Jermaine', that meat-head from / your gym

BETH. Don't call him that

TOBES. Why not?

BETH. He's a friend

TOBES. He's a meat-head

BETH. He's not a meat-head

TOBES. He does star-jumps for a living

BETH. And you sell pot plants. So

TOBES. So what?

BETH. So nothing

TOBES. I like my job

BETH. No you don't

TOBES. I do

BETH. You said yourself: it's a dead-end job with dead-end
    people, you said

TOBES. Is that why you're leaving me?

BETH. What? No

TOBES. You don't like my job?

BETH. You don't like your job! And it's nothing to do with that anyway

TOBES. What then?

BETH. It doesn't matter, Tobes

TOBES. Of course it does

BETH. I just. I don't

TOBES. But why?

BETH. Will you stop asking me that?

TOBES. You haven't given me an answer!

BETH. I have!

TOBES. But why?

BETH. It's not my job to fix you, Tobes

TOBES. To fix me?

BETH. To sort this out

TOBES. I didn't know I was broken

BETH. You're not

TOBES. Then what's. What's changed? I mean what's changed, / Beth?

BETH. Nothing! Nothing's changed, that's the problem, Tobes. Nothing has changed, at all, has it, since we got together. Really. Look at us and look at everyone else. We should've been somewhere by now, Tobes, moving forward. Moving *in* at least, we don't even live together

TOBES. Well if you want me to move in / I'll

BETH. I don't want you to move in

TOBES. Make up your mind!

BETH. I have. That's it. I'm sorry. I just. I want to get on with it now. My life. Change gear. Do things. Feel things. Do something spontaneous once in a while, instead of only ever going to the pub to watch the football

TOBES. We don't only ever go to the pub to watch / the

BETH. We did it yesterday

TOBES. It was the derby!

BETH. So?

TOBES. So it's important!

BETH. It's not important! Nothing about it is important

TOBES. We've just booked a holiday

BETH. I know

TOBES. For next month!

BETH. You can change the name on the / ticket

TOBES. Why did you let us book it?

BETH. I'll give you the money

TOBES. I don't want the money

BETH. I wasn't sure then, Tobes

TOBES. But now you are?

BETH....

TOBES. Well good for you

BETH. Don't hate me, Tobes

TOBES. I don't

BETH. Please don't

TOBES. I definitely don't hate you

BETH. This is hard for me too, Tobes, I'm not. I don't want to be the one who's hurting you

TOBES. Then don't. Don't do it, Beth

BETH. Tobes

TOBES. Please

BETH. It's done. Now please. For me, just. Man up a bit.

TOBES....

BETH. Sorry

TOBES. Man up a bit?

BETH. Ignore me, forget I said / that

TOBES. Man up?

BETH. No do what you want, it's your life.

TOBES *laughs/smiles*.

What

TOBES. No, just. My life.

BETH....

TOBES. Because a minute ago it was ours

BETH. I'm sorry, Tobes. I really am. I just. I don't

TOBES. Yeah I've got it now. Thanks

BETH. I'll miss you too. I will. I promise

TOBES. Is that my cue, then?

BETH....

TOBES. Alright. That's me. The end

BETH. The end

TOBES. Bye, Beth

BETH. Bye, Tobes

TOBES. Bye, Beth. Do you wanna get married?

BETH....

TOBES. Will you marry me, / Beth?

BETH. Tobes

TOBES. I'm only joking. I'll see you. Or not. Either way. That's me. Getting on with it.

Two

A staffroom.

TOBES *and* JARED, *his manager.*

JARED. You're late

TOBES. Sorry

JARED. What are you playing / at?

TOBES. Sorry

JARED. Sorry doesn't help me, does it? I've told you before. Sorry doesn't sell hedging. Or herbaceous perennials. Or Wimborne Bistro Sets

TOBES. I'm sorry, I just didn't really sleep and

JARED. Are you drunk?

TOBES. No

JARED. Have you been drinking?

TOBES. Yeah, a bit, yeah

JARED. It's half-ten in the morning

TOBES. I've only had a couple

JARED. You can't be drunk in here

TOBES. I'm not drunk

JARED. This is a place of business, you plank

TOBES. I just need to be busy, my, my, my, Beth, my

JARED. Beth?

TOBES. Yeah

JARED. Beth

TOBES. My. Yeah. We we sort of, we, / we

JARED. She's dumped you?

TOBES. No

JARED. She's binned you

TOBES. No, she

JARED. No?

TOBES. No it was a mutual thing

JARED. Is she shagging someone else?

TOBES. What? No!

JARED. Are you sure? Cos you were punching well above, there

TOBES. What?

JARED. You were. I'm not having a go. It's a compliment ennit?

TOBES. How is it?

JARED. You did well. You were together, what, six months?

TOBES. Two years

JARED. You didn't even live together

TOBES. I, no, I get mates' rates where I am, Billie gives me cheap rent

JARED. Still

TOBES. I don't get paid enough to move

JARED. Don't try and make this my fault

TOBES. I'm not, / I'm

JARED. You got dumped all on your own

TOBES. I didn't get dumped!

JARED. Alright, whatever, I don't care, / do I?

TOBES. It was mutual

JARED. What's the difference? It's over. Stop being such a delicate flower about it

TOBES. I'm not being a delicate flower

JARED. Well you are

TOBES. I'm not

JARED. You're being an orchid when you wanna be an oak tree

TOBES. I am an oak tree. That's exactly what I am

JARED. An oak tree'd be out there already looking for someone else to tend his acorns, not standing about in here on the verge of tears

TOBES. I'm not on the verge / of tears

JARED. Half-cut at half-ten in the morning

TOBES. I just need to be busy

JARED. You just need to get busy

TOBES. What?

JARED. You need to get your nuts up, that's all

TOBES. My. No I don't

JARED. What about that new girl with the glasses?

TOBES. No

JARED. Or your housemate, what's-her-name?

TOBES. Billie

JARED. Yeah. She's fit

TOBES. She's gay

JARED. Is she? Brilliant

TOBES. Why's / that

JARED. Or what about that girl from the chippy?

TOBES. No

JARED. Maxine

TOBES. Please

JARED. She's had a boob job

TOBES. Has she? No, look, no I don't care

JARED. You're not working. You shouldn't even be here with a drink inside you. What if there was a fire?

TOBES. What?

JARED. You'd go up like a Roman candle. I mean it. Go and get yourself laid. Move on. It's for your own good

TOBES. I can't just do that. Just go up to a girl and

JARED. You don't have to, mate. Two words: Tinder. One word

TOBES. Please

JARED. Look, I get it. You're worried. I don't blame you, you've been out of the game a while and fair enough, you're not what's-his-name. Harry Styles. Or even Harry Redknapp, but you're young, you've still got all your own teeth. You're not a monster, Tobes, someone'll sort you out. And anyway, you're not welcome here, so you might as well crack on, mightn't you?

TOBES....

JARED. Go on, hop it. Get out of my sight.

TOBES. Okay

JARED. And, Tobes, this is your last warning, alright? Next time you're out on your ear. Without a penny. You understand?

TOBES....

JARED. Go on then, chop-chop. And don't come back till someone's made you a man.

Three

ELLIE*'s bedroom.*

TOBES *and* ELLIE, *a girl from Tinder.*

ELLIE. What's wrong?

TOBES. Sorry, no, you just. For a second you looked like
   someone

ELLIE. Who?

TOBES. No, no one, just

ELLIE. Not like an ex or something?

TOBES. No. Well, yeah, but

ELLIE. Right. That's weird

TOBES. No yeah, it is a bit / but

ELLIE. Who's prettier?

TOBES....

ELLIE. Right well that's that then

TOBES. No, no sorry, you are

ELLIE. Don't bother

TOBES. No I mean it, / you're

ELLIE. Look, since we've stopped

TOBES. We don't have to

ELLIE. We've stopped. Can I ask you something?

TOBES. Well that sort of depends

ELLIE. I'm not trying to embarrass you but

TOBES....

ELLIE. How often do you check yourself?

TOBES. Sorry?

ELLIE. When was the last time you checked

TOBES. You mean my

ELLIE. Yeah your. Yeah

TOBES. For

ELLIE. Yeah, / for

TOBES. I don't, I don't, I mean whenever, really. All the time. Today, maybe? Probably today

ELLIE. Okay

TOBES. Why?

ELLIE. Just wondering

TOBES. Weird thing to wonder. In the middle of

ELLIE. We're not in the middle

TOBES. I can check *you* if, if you're worried about

ELLIE. No, it's you I'm.

TOBES. …

ELLIE. So you think it's alright then?

TOBES. …

ELLIE. That sort of. Lump.

Beat.

TOBES. That? That's. Yeah. That's. I mean. That's. Yeah

ELLIE. You've checked it out?

TOBES. It's a lump in a bag of lumps. I mean. It's normal

ELLIE. Is it though?

TOBES. It's been there ages, so

ELLIE. How long?

TOBES. I don't. Ages

ELLIE. But not forever?

TOBES. I mean no, but

ELLIE. It hasn't always been like that?

TOBES. It's not 'like' anything

ELLIE. Have you had it checked?

TOBES. It's, yeah it's fine

ELLIE. Have you had it checked?

TOBES. Yeah

ELLIE. Have you?

TOBES. No, but

ELLIE. No?

TOBES. There's nothing wrong with it, so

ELLIE. How do you know?

TOBES. I'm not being funny, I've seen a lot more of them than
    you have, so

ELLIE. So?

TOBES. So I mean, don't worry about it

ELLIE. Is it getting bigger?

TOBES. No!

ELLIE. Are you sure? You're a high-risk group

TOBES. I'm. What? I know / I'm

ELLIE. It's rife in men your age

TOBES. I know it is

ELLIE. It happens all the time

TOBES. I know

ELLIE. People die

TOBES. Alright, you've made your point, will you leave it now?!

ELLIE.…

TOBES. I'm sorry, but

ELLIE. Do you want to have sex?

Beat.

TOBES. Yeah. Yes please

ELLIE. Not now. Ever.

TOBES....

ELLIE. Go and get it looked at

TOBES. This is bizarre

ELLIE. What is?

TOBES. 'I'll only shag you if you get your balls checked'?

ELLIE. I'm not gonna shag you after this

TOBES. Alright

ELLIE. I just don't want you to end up like a freak. You could be like that Channel 4 documentary

TOBES. What documentary?

ELLIE. The man with the ten-tonne.

TOBES....

ELLIE. You know the one

TOBES. I must've missed it. Any good?

ELLIE. It was one of the most depressing things I've ever seen

TOBES. Right. Yeah. I suppose it would be.

ELLIE....

TOBES. You really think it's weird then?

ELLIE. Yeah

TOBES. Like I should worry about it?

ELLIE. No, like you should get it looked at.

TOBES....

ELLIE. I'm not a doctor. It might be nothing

TOBES. Or I might be a Channel 4 documentary

ELLIE. Well.

Beat.

TOBES. Fifteen minutes of fame at least!

Beat.

ELLIE. You should really watch this thing

TOBES. Yeah I probably should

ELLIE. At home, maybe.

Beat.

TOBES. Right.

ELLIE....

TOBES. Yeah.

ELLIE....

TOBES. Well I'll see myself out.

Four

A hallway.

TOBES *and* JOFF, *his best mate.*

JOFF. Tobes

TOBES. I need a favour

JOFF. Right

TOBES. It's pretty massive

JOFF. I haven't got any money

TOBES. When have I ever asked you for money?

JOFF. That's why it'd be massive

TOBES. I don't want your money

JOFF. Good, cos I haven't got any

TOBES. I know. Listen

Beat.

JOFF. Go on then

TOBES. Is Liza in?

JOFF. Is.

TOBES....

JOFF. It's two o'clock in the morning, Tobes. She's in bed

TOBES. Sorry. How is she?

JOFF. How is she?

TOBES. How's she doing?

JOFF. She's asleep

TOBES. No I mean. You know, the bump and

JOFF. Well there isn't one yet, but

TOBES. No, but

JOFF. Yeah it's good. I mean it's early days, / but

TOBES. I'm happy for you, mate, really. I dunno if I've said
that yet. I mean I wasn't sure when you told me, I'll be
honest, I was a bit like: it's pretty soon. And I mean we're
still just kids ourselves, aren't we? But we're not, are we,
really, people die younger than us

JOFF. What you going on about, Tobes? What do you need?

TOBES....

JOFF. Spit it out, come on!

TOBES. I need you to feel my balls.

JOFF....

TOBES. Please

JOFF. What?

TOBES. I need a second opinion

JOFF. What?

TOBES. It's only one. There's a little. Something

JOFF. Go and see a doctor, man!

TOBES. I can't

JOFF. Why not?

TOBES. They'll be closed

JOFF. Well now, yeah, but

TOBES. And I've had the same one since we were six

JOFF. Dr Azad?

TOBES. Exactly. Him. I can't just go / and

JOFF. He's alright

TOBES. No I know, but he gave me my asthma pump

JOFF. So?

TOBES. So he used to give me a sticker for being good. I don't
    want to drop my pants in front of him

JOFF. He might give you two stickers

TOBES. Joff!

JOFF. Sorry

TOBES. This is

JOFF. You want me to feel your balls?

TOBES. I don't *want* you to, but. Yeah. I mean. What choice
    have I got?

JOFF. Dr Azad!

TOBES. Please, Joff, you've seen them before

JOFF. Across the room in the showers, yeah

TOBES. Remember when your brother put that fishing rod
    through your foot?

JOFF. Don't try / and

TOBES. I took it apart and carried you to the hospital piggyback

JOFF. You can't compare that / to

TOBES. Please Joff

JOFF. This is a living nightmare

TOBES. Please. It'll take two seconds

JOFF. That's all you're getting.

TOBES....

JOFF. Come on then. Drop trou

TOBES. What, here? What if Liza comes in?

JOFF. Then I'll kill myself. Come on

TOBES. Can't you just. Dip in?

JOFF. For ffff

TOBES. Yeah, I know. I'm sorry

JOFF. If you're having me on

TOBES. I'm. No! Why would I?

JOFF. You can't tell anyone this ever happened

TOBES. Trust me

JOFF. Which one is it?

TOBES. The left

JOFF. Alright. Come on then.

TOBES....

JOFF. You ready?

TOBES. Is your hand cold?

JOFF. I'm not warming it up for you

TOBES. Alright.

The two men look at each other. Deep breaths.

Then JOFF *slides his hand in.* TOBES *flinches, but soon they've settled in, grimly.*

Another beat and JOFF *pulls his hand out again.*

What do you think?

JOFF. That's the worst thing I've ever done

TOBES. Does it feel alright?

JOFF. Yeah it's fine. I need to wash my hand

TOBES. Thanks, mate, thank you, so much. I'll buy you a pint. Or ten. There's football on tomorrow / night

JOFF. I don't think that's right

TOBES. Seven forty-five, it's on Sky

JOFF. No, I mean

TOBES. But you just said

JOFF. I know, but

TOBES. Oh no, no, no, no, no, no, no

JOFF. How long's that been there, Tobes? How long's / that

TOBES. A while

JOFF. How long?

TOBES. A year maybe?

JOFF. A year?

TOBES. Longer

JOFF. Tobes, go to Dr Azad. First thing tomorrow

TOBES. I've got work

JOFF. Forget work

TOBES. My rent's due / in

JOFF. What's more important? Tomorrow morning, Tobes

TOBES. Alright, I will

JOFF. Do

TOBES. Yeah, I will. I will. I will. I will.

Beat.

Joff, if I die, will / you

JOFF. You're not gonna die

TOBES. If I do will you name the baby after me?

Beat.

JOFF. No.

TOBES....

JOFF. Be weird, wouldn't it? 'Tobes is dead, but that's alright we've got a new Tobes, so'

TOBES....

JOFF. I'll die before you anyway. My family's got a history of strokes.

Beat.

Tobes?

TOBES. Yeah?

JOFF. You'll be alright

TOBES. Will I?

JOFF. I dunno. But. Can I leave you on your own for a minute? I really need to go and wash my hand.

Five

A GP's surgery.

TOBES *and* LILY, *a GP.*

LILY. Come in, come in, come in

TOBES. Are you the doctor?

LILY. Ha! I always feel like David Tennant when people ask
    me that

TOBES. You feel / like

LILY. I know he's not been on it for ages, but. Y'know. Who is
    it now?

TOBES. You mean Doctor Who?

LILY. Yeah

TOBES. No idea

LILY. Not a fan?

TOBES. I've never watched it

LILY. No nor have I, really. Funny. Because it's huge, isn't it?
    Anyway ignore me. Sorry. Sit down. What can we do for you?

TOBES. What happened to Dr Azad?

LILY. He regenerated

TOBES. What?

LILY. Sorry, still on Doctor Who. My nephews like it. No he
    retired, actually. Moved to Nottingham I think

TOBES. Nottingham?

LILY. His son was studying there, if memory serves. So now
    it's me. So. What seems to be the problem?

TOBES. Can I ask, are there any.

LILY....

TOBES. I'm not being rude. Are you the only one available?
    Doctor

LILY. I'm afraid so

TOBES. There's no

LILY. No

TOBES. Men?

LILY. Not today, sorry

TOBES. Okay, and there's no one

LILY. No one

TOBES. Less

LILY....

TOBES. Fit?

LILY. Oh

TOBES. Sorry

LILY. No, I wasn't expecting that

TOBES. Nor was I, I thought you'd be Dr Azad

LILY. Well no, I'm. No. That's nice of you to say, but no, I'm the only one here today

TOBES. Okay

LILY. But I promise my being a woman won't affect anything

TOBES. I mean it might

LILY. There's nothing I won't have seen before.

TOBES....

LILY. There is a male doctor in on Friday mornings if you'd / rather

TOBES. No I'll. No. It's taken me years to come this time, so

LILY. Years? Okay. So how can I help?

   Long beat.

   Would you like to write down what the problem is?

TOBES. No, it's

Long beat.

LILY. Is it below your waist?

TOBES....

LILY. To do with your penis?

TOBES....

LILY. Or scrotum?

TOBES....

LILY. Okay. So do you think you might have an STI or?

TOBES. No! I'm. No, I'm careful. I mean I've actually only had one girlfriend, so. One proper girlfriend, I mean. When I was a kid I had girlfriends, but. Not, like. I sort of started late, really, so Beth's sort of it as far as

LILY. Okay. So what seems to be the problem?

TOBES....

LILY. Tell you what: why don't you just pop your trousers down and we can have a little look at what we're dealing with?

TOBES. Are you seeing anyone?

LILY....

TOBES. I mean have you got a boyfriend? Because I haven't. A girlfriend I mean. And I think I might find it easier if you have. Somehow. So I know there's no. Chance, or

LILY. Right

TOBES. Sorry

LILY. Yeah. Yes. I have

TOBES. Have you?

LILY. We've just got engaged, actually

TOBES. Really? Right. Okay. Well, that's. Congratulations

LILY. Thanks. Thank you

TOBES. Really, that's

LILY. We're actually meeting for lunch in

TOBES. Oh sorry

LILY. No it's / fine

TOBES. Lunch? What time is it?

LILY. Midday?

TOBES. What?

LILY. Twelve o'clock

TOBES. Really? How's. I am so late for work

LILY. Okay, well

TOBES. It's a lump. A bump

LILY. I see

TOBES. On, on, on my left

LILY. I'm with you. Say no more. I'll give it a squeeze and see what we're dealing with

TOBES. If it is. Something. I'd know, wouldn't I? I mean I feel like I would know

LILY. It's hard to say

TOBES. But people must know, don't they? You can't just walk around

LILY. It depends

TOBES. On what?

LILY. On lots of things

TOBES. I feel fine, that's the thing. And nothing much has changed. Not really. So I mean, that's good. Isn't it? That's positive

LILY. It's impossible to say without us having a look, but you know you really should've come to us straight away

TOBES. Dr Azad gave me my asthma pump

LILY. Sorry?

TOBES. I used to come here when I was little. I've always come here

LILY. There are clinics you can go to. Drop-ins. GUMs. Anyway, you're here now, so let's try and put your mind at rest. Trousers and pants around your ankles

TOBES. If we met. Out somewhere. In the street. Or in a bar. Or, or on Tinder or. And you didn't have a boyf. A fiancé. What's his name?

LILY. John

TOBES. If you didn't have a John and I wasn't about to take my trousers off

LILY. I'm not sure / I

TOBES. My girlfriend left me a couple of days ago

LILY. Right

TOBES. And then I joined Tinder and it wasn't exactly

LILY....

TOBES. You're not wearing a ring. An engagement ring

LILY. I don't really believe in them, / so

TOBES. Okay. You didn't just make John up?

LILY. No

TOBES. Okay. Sorry. Thank you. You're lovely. Sorry. I've just I've had a few drinks. I'll shut up now

LILY. If you could just pop your trousers off, / then

TOBES. Sorry. Absolutely, yeah. I'll get my balls out now.

Six

An office in a hospital.

TOBES *and* JULIAN, *a medical consultant.*

JULIAN. Would you like to sit down?

TOBES. I don't know yet

JULIAN. Okay

TOBES. How old are you?

JULIAN. I'm. Sorry?

TOBES. You're really a consultant?

JULIAN. Newly qualified, actually, but

TOBES. Well done. I'm on my last warning at a garden centre

    JULIAN *smiles sympathetically.*

    What's that?

JULIAN. What's

TOBES. That. That smile

JULIAN. Nothing

TOBES. Oh

JULIAN. Nothing, just / a smile

TOBES. Ohhhhhhhhhhhhhhh. Oh no. Alright, alright, okay, alright, um. Yeah. Alright. Do I need to be here?

JULIAN. Sorry?

TOBES. Do I need to stay here?

JULIAN. For the moment, / yes

TOBES. Why?

JULIAN. We need to have a chat about your

TOBES. But do we though? I mean I know, I can tell by your face, so you've told me, so do I need to stay here or can I actually just go home and wait for a letter or whatever about whatever happens next? A pamphlet maybe

JULIAN. No, I need to take you through

TOBES. I need to go, I've got to tell my mum

JULIAN. I'm afraid you can't, just yet

TOBES. Why not?

JULIAN. I need to take you through

TOBES. You're not listening. Why are you not listening? What happened to the other one?

JULIAN. The other

TOBES. Consultant. The one I saw before

JULIAN. Mr Fourie

TOBES. The older one

JULIAN. Jaako

TOBES. The adult

JULIAN. He's actually he's on a round-the-world cruise at the moment

TOBES. He's what?

JULIAN. He's on his holidays

TOBES. Oh what an absolute, complete and utter

JULIAN. Now I'll stop you there

TOBES. Oh will you now?

JULIAN. I know this is stressful, / but

TOBES. Do you?

JULIAN. There's no need to be offensive

TOBES. What? You think I'm being offensive?

JULIAN. Well you were about to swear and

TOBES. Jesus, wouldn't you? I mean think about it you, / you

JULIAN. Toby

TOBES. That's not my name

JULIAN. Tobin

TOBES. And no one calls me that

JULIAN. Mr Piper

TOBES. They made you a consultant?!

JULIAN. Yes / they

TOBES. You've got the bedside manner of a sex offender

JULIAN. And you've got the attitude of, of, of

TOBES. Of what? Of

JULIAN. Nothing, look, listen to get back to the point: we
    don't know for certain that what we think is unfriendly here
    is in fact

TOBES. Unfriendly?

JULIAN. Sinister

TOBES. It's not a Bond villain!

JULIAN. No, look, the fact of the matter is your bloods came
    back negative and there's nothing to suggest mestastisation
    anywhere so it might be that actually, yes, we're dealing with
    something benign

TOBES. Benign?

JULIAN. Or it might be that we've caught it early. But,
    unfortunately, because of the region and the surface area
    we're dealing with there is a high risk of spreading
    malignant spores / if

TOBES. In English please

JULIAN. We need to do more tests, but we can't biopsy your
    lump in situ, nor can we remove it on its own.

    Beat.

TOBES. You wanna take my balls off

JULIAN. Not exactly, no. We would like to remove the
    troubling one, / but

TOBES. I don't want it done

JULIAN. I know. I know the thought of it is

TOBES. You don't know anything about the thought of it

JULIAN. I've seen this operation performed a hundred times

TOBES. And how many have you had off yourself?

JULIAN. Well, none

TOBES. So what could you possibly know about it?

JULIAN. …

TOBES. Answer me! What do you actually know about it?

JULIAN. Look I can see you're distressed and I don't blame
    you, but I will have to call security if you / keep

TOBES. What for? You can't kick me out. You've taken an
    oath, you've got to treat me no matter what

JULIAN. You've already told me you don't want the operation

TOBES. I don't want to die either, do I?!

JULIAN. No. You don't.

TOBES. …

JULIAN. Look. For what it's worth: the chances are it won't
    affect your fertility and / we

TOBES. The chances are?

JULIAN. We can offer you a prosthetic replacement for
    cosmetic purposes if you decide that's something you want.
    But if we leave it alone and it is what we think it is

TOBES. …

JULIAN. I'm going to arrange an appointment for you to make
    a sperm donation

TOBES. Jesus

JULIAN. And you'll receive a letter within the week with a date
    and time for your orchidectomy

TOBES. My orchid

JULIAN. Orchidectomy. That's what it's called. Okay?

TOBES. No, not 'okay', not even nearly okay, just let me think about it

JULIAN. We would strongly advise

TOBES. I know what you'd advise!

JULIAN. Alright. Well that's it. You can go now, Mr Piper.

TOBES....

JULIAN. You can leave. We'll be in touch

TOBES. I'm sorry

JULIAN. It's fine, but I have other people to see

TOBES. I am. I'm sorry. I've barely ever even had a cold

JULIAN. I understand

TOBES. Will you tell me something nice? Please?

JULIAN....

TOBES. Just something good?

Beat.

JULIAN. My dog died this morning.

TOBES....

JULIAN. I say died, I had to take her to be put down. So. No. I don't think I've got it in me. Sorry.

TOBES....

JULIAN. You should have the operation.

Seven

A living room.

TOBES *and* LISE, *his sister.*

LISE. Look who it isn't

TOBES. What are you doing here?

LISE. I'm house-sitting, aren't I

TOBES. Where's Mum?

LISE. Gone up to look after Nan. You know / this

TOBES. For how long?

LISE. You know all about this, Tobes

TOBES. Alright

LISE. What do you want her for?

TOBES. Nothing

LISE. What?

TOBES. Nothing, no, just. I need to talk to her

LISE. About

TOBES. I just I need to tell her something

LISE. What?

TOBES. Nothing

LISE. What, Tobes?

TOBES. No nothing

LISE. What do you need to tell her?

Beat.

TOBES. I need to borrow some money. That's all

LISE. You what? You need to borrow money?

TOBES. Yeah, just

LISE. Why?

TOBES. Take a wild guess

LISE. I'm asking you

TOBES. My rent's due / so

LISE. Why can't you use your own money?

TOBES. Because I haven't got any

LISE. Obviously, but why?

TOBES. I just. I bought a holiday, so. Me and Beth are going away and

LISE. You are unbelievable

TOBES. What?

LISE. You are unbelievable, do you know that?

TOBES. Why?

LISE. Why?! I mean where do I start? It doesn't only affect you, you know. We're family, Tobes

TOBES....

LISE. Why didn't you tell me?

TOBES. What?

LISE. Why didn't you tell me, Tobes? I had to hear it from Jack this morning

TOBES. Jack?

LISE. Yeah

TOBES. Jack?

LISE. I know: he's supposed to be the idiot brother, and yet somehow you've managed to overtake him

TOBES. How does he even. What? How does Jack know / about

LISE. They're at the same gym, aren't they?

TOBES....

LISE. They do spin together

TOBES. Who does? What?

LISE. Jack does

TOBES. What are you talking about?

LISE. You and Beth. Splitting up. What, a fortnight ago? And
I find out this morning from Jack. What did you think
I wouldn't care? I do. I do care, I liked Beth. I still like her,
a lot. I mean I thought that was it. I thought you two might

TOBES. Yeah

LISE. She's pretty and funny and bright and, and cultured / and

TOBES. I know

LISE. And worldly. She's got it all going for her, Tobes. She's
a winner

TOBES. Yep

LISE. So? What happened?

TOBES. I did

LISE. What?

TOBES. Nothing, no, just. We. I don't know

LISE. You don't know?

TOBES. Not really, no

LISE. You must know

TOBES. She didn't really say much, so

LISE. What, so she left you? She dumped you?

TOBES. I mean it was her idea, if that's, I mean, if that's, yeah,
if you want. She left me. Dumped me. Chucked me. Off
a cliff, actually, so, yeah. She did. From a great height, so

LISE. So why didn't you tell me, Tobes?

TOBES. I've just I've been a bit busy

LISE. With?

TOBES. Nothing, just. Work and

LISE. Work?

TOBES. Yeah

LISE. Work

TOBES. Yeah, overtime / and

LISE. I went down to your work this morning, Tobes

TOBES. Why?

LISE. Because. Your phone was off. And like I said, I care. You weren't there. You've been sacked, Tobes

TOBES. Yeah. I know

LISE. For turning up blind drunk and hours late

TOBES. I wasn't drunk

LISE. And now you want to come here and borrow money? What's going on, Tobes?

TOBES....

LISE. Are you depressed or something?

TOBES. No

LISE. Is that why you're drinking?

TOBES. I'm not depressed, I'm

LISE. What?

TOBES. I'm, I'm, I'm fine

LISE. You're not fine, / Tobes

TOBES. I am. I'm fine

LISE. You're a mess. You look like the sky's fallen on your head

TOBES. Yeah well I feel like it

LISE. So do something about it

TOBES. I am

LISE. Like what?

TOBES. I'm getting on with it

LISE. By drinking in the daytime? And borrowing money?

TOBES. Look I don't need a lecture, alright?

LISE. I think you do

TOBES. No, what I need is rent. So can you lend me it or not?

LISE. Me? No!

TOBES. Alright, fine

LISE. And don't go asking Mum either; she's done enough for
   you already. You got yourself into this mess, so you can get
   yourself out

TOBES. Did I, really?

LISE. What?

TOBES. Get myself into this?

LISE. Who else did it? It's up to you. What else is there, Tobes?

TOBES. ...

LISE. What else is there?

TOBES. Nothing

LISE. Exactly. So sort it out.

Eight

A travel shop.

TOBES *and* JUSTIN, *a travel agent.*

JUSTIN. Yes, sir

TOBES. I need a refund. Please. I sort of lost my job and

JUSTIN. Oh no, I'm so sorry to hear that

TOBES. No no it's fine. Well I mean it's not but that's, that's not, that's the least of my worries, I just I booked this thing a few weeks ago but now I need the money, so

JUSTIN. Ah well the problem is

TOBES. I know there's probably a charge or whatever, but

JUSTIN. Well

TOBES. Whatever you can give me

JUSTIN. We don't do refunds, I'm afraid.

   Beat.

TOBES. What?

JUSTIN. That's the policy. Our flights are non-refundable

TOBES. You don't do refunds?

JUSTIN. Sorry

TOBES. You can't not do refunds

JUSTIN. Well

TOBES. Just not do

JUSTIN. We don't, I'm afraid

TOBES. Why not?

JUSTIN. It's just. It's company policy, sir

TOBES. To steal money from people?

JUSTIN. To. No, to

TOBES. To

JUSTIN. The policy should have been made clear to you when you booked

TOBES. Well it wasn't

JUSTIN. Okay. Well. Okay. Well I'm sorry about that. But it should have been in the confirmation email we sent you

TOBES. And what if it wasn't?

JUSTIN. Um. Well. It was. / So

TOBES. It wasn't

JUSTIN. Okay, well. It was definitely on the forms you signed on the day

TOBES. No it wasn't

JUSTIN. I can promise you. They're all the same

TOBES. It wasn't on there

JUSTIN. I can go and get them, / if

TOBES. Are you calling me a liar?

JUSTIN. No, I'm. No

TOBES. It wasn't on there.

Beat.

JUSTIN. I'll just go and get our copies of the forms

TOBES. What for?

JUSTIN. To prove

TOBES. It doesn't matter. Things have changed, I need a refund

JUSTIN. Okay, well, I understand / but

TOBES. No you don't. You don't understand

JUSTIN. Okay

TOBES. I need a refund

JUSTIN. Okay

TOBES. So give me a refund

JUSTIN. Okay, okay, okay

TOBES. Thank you

JUSTIN. No I wasn't, no, look, listen, sir, our cancellations policy doesn't cater for changes in employment

TOBES. What does it cater for?

JUSTIN. Well not much

TOBES. Does it cater for terminal illness? For example

JUSTIN. As I say: essentially we don't do refunds

TOBES. Essentially?

JUSTIN. In essence

TOBES. I know what essentially means

JUSTIN. You do actually have ten days from the point of booking to amend or cancel / if

TOBES. So you do do refunds?

JUSTIN. In a sense

TOBES. In the sense that you do do them

JUSTIN. Within the first ten days

TOBES. So then pretend this is the first ten days

JUSTIN. But it's not, is it?

TOBES. That's why you have to pretend!

JUSTIN. Then there's really nothing I can do

TOBES. You really can!

JUSTIN. Our policy does state

TOBES. If you say that one more time

JUSTIN. My hands are tied

TOBES. Alright, I want to see your manager

JUSTIN. I'm, that's me, I am the manager

TOBES. You're the manager?

JUSTIN. I'm afraid so. Sorry.

TOBES. Are you? Sorry? Because you should be

JUSTIN. I don't make the rules, / sir

TOBES. You've said. A hundred times. It's policy

JUSTIN. It is

TOBES. Is this what your life is? Policy and I-don't-make-the-rules and yes-sir-no-sir-three-bags-full-sir? Working here, in a dead-end job with dead-end people selling plastic happiness to desperate idiots? Don't you just get home sometimes and take a look in the mirror and think 'what a complete-and-utter waste of time and effort and energy and oxygen'?

JUSTIN. No. I don't

TOBES. You probably should

JUSTIN. I like my job. Usually. When you're not in it. So. No I don't think I am a waste of time and effort and energy, I make people happy. Give them something to look forward to. And even if I didn't: it pays the bills, doesn't it? Keeps me in clothes, lets me go to the cinema, or whatever. It's a job, at the end of the day. I've got a job. What have you got?

TOBES. You wanna know what I've got?

TOBES *tries, but he can't say it.*

Long beat.

JUSTIN. I thought as much.

Beat.

If I were you I'd take myself on holiday.

Nine

A sperm bank.

TOBES *and* BESS, *a medical receptionist.*

BESS. Can I help?

TOBES. I think I need a hand

BESS. A hand?

TOBES. Or something. Not a hand, I didn't mean / a

BESS. We don't do that here

TOBES. Sorry, no, slip of the tongue

BESS. Or that. Unless you buy us dinner first.

TOBES. ...

BESS. I'm joking. This is a clinic, not a brothel

TOBES. Sorry, yeah, I'm gonna start again

BESS. Please do

TOBES. It's.

BESS. ...

TOBES. It's not working

BESS. What's not working?

TOBES. The stuff

BESS. The stuff?

TOBES. The, yeah, the stuff

BESS. Okay

TOBES. I can't seem / to

BESS. What stuff?

TOBES. The, the, the stuff, the

BESS. Oh

TOBES. The

BESS. Right. I'm with you

TOBES. It's not. It's not. I can't

BESS. You can't achieve an erection?

TOBES. I mean it's impossible, surely? In that room? With those magazines and. The pressure of. Well anyway, there's a sign on the wall. It says to come and find someone if

BESS....

TOBES. 'If you have any problems please contact a member of staff'

BESS. Okay

TOBES. Something like that

BESS. That sort of means if the door won't lock, or if the light goes out or

TOBES. Right

BESS. Or if you miss the cup or something

TOBES. Yeah of course it. Sorry

BESS. You haven't missed the cup, have you?

TOBES. No

BESS. Good. Cos I really don't get paid enough / to

TOBES. I haven't even come close to. No. It's just. The stuff

BESS. Are you telling me you need gay porn? Because we don't do that

TOBES. No

BESS. It's still considered niche

TOBES. I don't need

BESS. Backward I know, / but

TOBES. I don't need gay porn, just. Something newer, maybe?

BESS. This isn't Waterstones

TOBES. I know, but. Just. Is there anything else in the other rooms, maybe?

BESS. All the rooms are in use at the moment

TOBES. Okay

BESS. And to be honest, most people just use their phones anyway

TOBES. Okay, the problem with that is my mum pays my phone bill. And. I don't know if it's itemised / or

BESS. Your mum pays your phone bill?

TOBES. Yeah. She bought me the phone. Years ago. It was in her name and I never switched it over, / so

BESS. So your mum pays your phone bill every month?

TOBES. Yeah

BESS. Since

TOBES. Since quite a while, yeah

BESS. Is she rich?

TOBES. Not at all, / no

BESS. Then what?

TOBES. Sorry we're sort of getting off the point

BESS. Think of all the money you must have saved

TOBES. My rent's due and I haven't got it, so

BESS. Still

TOBES. It hasn't helped that much

BESS. I wish my mum paid my phone bill

TOBES. Well it means you can't use your phone to look at porn, / so

BESS. I don't look at porn

TOBES. Okay

BESS. I think it's fundamentally demeaning to women.

   Beat.

TOBES. Okay. Sorry

BESS. It's not your fault

TOBES. No, but

BESS. Not all your fault anyway

TOBES. Is there really nothing else I could use?

BESS. Your imagination?

TOBES....

BESS. I'm not being funny. Have you got a girlfriend? Or a boyfriend?

TOBES. No, I'm not

BESS. Or an ex?

TOBES. I've. Yeah I've got / an

BESS. So pick a memory with them. Use that

TOBES. I can't

BESS. Why not?

TOBES. It's just a bit. I dunno

BESS. Did she dump you?

TOBES. No, it was mutual, / but

BESS. Was she sleeping with someone else?

TOBES. Why do people keep. No, it's just. It's too soon

BESS. If you say so

TOBES. Can I just take the cup away with me, maybe?

BESS. Doesn't work like that

TOBES. Or I could come back later on? When I've got something else to look at? Tomorrow, even

BESS. We're fully booked until next Monday. You could come back then

TOBES. No, it'll be too late by then, I'll have had my

BESS....

TOBES. I'll have had

Beat.

BESS. You mean you'll have had / your

TOBES. I think I need to sit down

BESS. Okay.

Long beat.

You're still standing up

TOBES. I don't really know how

Beat.

BESS. Look I'm sure your mum'll understand, won't she? In the circumstances

TOBES. She doesn't know. So

BESS. What?

TOBES. Not yet

BESS. Your mum doesn't know that you've got

TOBES. No

BESS. Why?

TOBES. She's got a lot on, so

BESS. Bigger than this?

TOBES. My nan's on her own and. Struggling. She's gone to help her out

BESS. Don't you think she might want to know?

TOBES. Maybe, / but

BESS. I think I'd want to know if it was my son

TOBES. It's not though, is it? It's me. It's my problem and I'll sort it out on my own

BESS. Why?

TOBES. Because I can. Because I should. Because I'm a man

BESS. Because you're a man?

TOBES. Exactly

BESS. You know how that one ends? With them scraping you off a pavement somewhere. Trust me. I've seen it all before. Tell someone, or don't expect a happy ending.

TOBES....

BESS. Speaking of which: you've only got that room for five more minutes.

Ten

A hospital waiting area.

TOBES *and his brother,* JACK.

JACK. Good news that the boys can swim, like.

TOBES....

JACK. Tobes.

TOBES....

JACK. Lads.

TOBES....

JACK. Little tadpole lads.

TOBES....

JACK. Tads.

TOBES....

JACK. Did they give you stuff to look at? Material

TOBES....

JACK. Tobes. At the thing. The other day

TOBES *nods*.

I bet it's all from the eighties, ennit. All massive bushes and cigarettes. Pages stuck together and that. Is it?

TOBES. Pretty much

JACK. You should've used your phone. That's what I'd have done I reckon. I've got some stuff on there.

Beat.

You remember that girl with the eyebrows? We went out for a bit. I met her on a train.

TOBES....

JACK. Danish

TOBES....

JACK. Polish

TOBES. What about her?

JACK. She's on there. Couple of videos

TOBES....

JACK. What?

TOBES. You can't have seen her in about a year, Jack

JACK. So? They were a present. I didn't give her back them trainers, did I?

TOBES....

JACK. I bet you've still got stuff with Beth on your phone

TOBES. No

JACK. Like you never made any

TOBES. I'm not talking about this

JACK. Shame about you and her, Tobes. She was fit

TOBES. Yeah, thanks

JACK. You wanna see her leg drive on the bike. At spin.
Powerful.

TOBES....

JACK. I'm not in these films by the way. On my phone. With
Elsa

TOBES. I don't want to know

JACK. Not my face anyway.

Beat.

What time is it now?

TOBES. Ten-to

JACK. Dragging ennit?

TOBES....

JACK. Did they tell you how long it takes?

TOBES....

JACK. Tobes?

TOBES. I can't remember

JACK. And do they keep you in?

TOBES. I don't know

JACK. You don't know?

TOBES. It depends

JACK. On what?

TOBES. I don't. How well it goes, I suppose

JACK. So you could be out tonight, then? Cos you know we're
on BT Sport? Should be a good one as well, they've got their
striker back, apparently. What's-his-name, with the haircut.
Spanish. Something. What d'you think? Do you think we'll
win? Be a close one, I reckon, with them having the
Spaniard back; he's quick. And we could do with a new
centre-half, couldn't we, really? Someone a bit more mobile.

More dynamic or something. But then you've been saying that for ages haven't you? And it's getting worse, I tell you, our offside trap looked like the tide coming in last week, did you see it? It was like watching in slow motion

TOBES. Jack, do me a favour. Shut up a minute.

Long beat.

JACK. Mum gets in at six. I'm picking her up from the station

TOBES. Don't bring her here. Please. I don't want her here

JACK. How come?

TOBES. I just. I spoke to her again this morning and all she did was cry

JACK. Lise said you told her not to come as well

TOBES. I did. She's even worse

JACK. Fair do's. Fair play. Lads day out then, eh?

TOBES. ...

JACK. It's a joke, Tobes

TOBES. Yeah

JACK. Just trying to lighten the mood

TOBES. Well don't, just. Let's just sit here, shall we?

JACK. Whatever you want.

Long beat.

So what do you reckon, Tobes? You think we'll win tonight?

TOBES. What is wrong with you?

JACK. ...

TOBES. Can you hear yourself? It's like you stopped at puberty, Jack. Listen to yourself, it's just noise. No one cares. It's not important. No one cares about the football or the girls you've shagged or the fights you've had or that goal you scored from the halfway line when you were in Year 11. It doesn't matter. It doesn't make you any more of a man, if that's what you

think. It makes you a moron. It's boring, Jack. You're boring.
I mean. Get on with it. Grow up, will you? Jesus

JACK. Are you finished?

TOBES....

JACK. Are you finished, / Tobes?

TOBES. Look, I'm saying this for you

JACK. Well thanks. No, really, thanks a lot, I appreciate it.
What a lovely thing to do, to try and help me out like that.
But I tell you what: you're lucky you're already in hospital,
or I might have put you there myself.

Beat.

TOBES. I think you'd better go now

JACK. Look

TOBES. Now, Jack

JACK. Alright, alright, alright, alright, alright, alright, alright.

TOBES....

JACK. Alright. Gimme a ring if you want picking up later,
yeah?

TOBES. I won't

JACK. Alright, walk home, whatever. I'll see you later, then.
Good luck, yeah?

TOBES....

JACK. Bye then.

JACK *goes.*

TOBES. Yeah.

TOBES *puts his hands down his pants and cradles his
testicles.*

Bye then.

Eleven

An operating theatre.

Sound and fury.

TOBES *has his left testicle removed.*

Twelve

TOBES*'s room.*

TOBES *and his flatmate,* BILLIE.

BILLIE. Have you got everything you need?

Beat.

TOBES. Have I got everything I need?

BILLIE. I just meant. Supplies or whatever. Lucozade. White
bread. Ice cream

TOBES. I haven't had my tonsils out

BILLIE. No, I know, but.

TOBES....

BILLIE. Something nice.

Beat.

I thought you might be back last night.

TOBES. Yeah.

BILLIE. Or this morning at least

TOBES. Turns out I don't heal well, so

BILLIE. Right

TOBES. Surprise surprise

BILLIE. Does it hurt?

Beat.

TOBES *nods*.

A lot?

TOBES *shakes his head*.

Okay. And did they tell you anything?

About. Y'know. If that's it, / or

TOBES. They'll phone me

BILLIE. Today? Tomorrow?

TOBES. Was there something you wanted, Billie? In particular,
I mean or

BILLIE. No, just. Saying hello

TOBES. Then, sorry, / but

BILLIE. Actually, there is something, Tobes.

TOBES....

BILLIE. I need your money

TOBES. What?

BILLIE. Your rent. I know, I'm sorry, it's not me, it's my dad,
he's going nuts, he keeps saying he'll come round and pack
up your stuff himself if he has to, and he means it, Tobes,
he's up a height, he's got this tax bill to pay / and

TOBES. Are you kicking me out?

BILLIE. No

TOBES. Now?

BILLIE. I'm not kicking you out

TOBES. Your dad's gonna come and pack up my stuff

BILLIE. No, he wants you to stay, / but

TOBES. I've been in hospital, Bill!

BILLIE. I know you have

TOBES. I've just had a part of me removed, for Christ's sake!

BILLIE. It was late already, Tobes, come on, you know it was, and it's not like this is first time either

TOBES. I've never once not paid you

BILLIE. Eventually, yeah / but

TOBES. So wait. Tell your dad to wait

BILLIE. He can't. And things have changed, haven't they, you don't have an income any more

TOBES. And I might be dying

BILLIE. Well, no, not that

TOBES. I might not be here next month to pay it back

BILLIE. You're not gonna die, Tobes

TOBES. I might though mightn't I!

BILLIE. Look I know this is scary stuff

TOBES. No you don't. Why do people keep saying they know? You don't know. You don't understand, / Billie

BILLIE. Alright, you're right, I don't. I can't imagine what it's like, but I'm not the enemy, Tobes, I'm on your side

TOBES. You've got a funny way of showing it

BILLIE. It's money, that's all. Just borrow it from someone and then

TOBES. Like who?

BILLIE. I don't know, your family?

TOBES. I can't

BILLIE. Or Joff?

TOBES. He hasn't got any

BILLIE. Then get a loan. A proper one

TOBES. Who's gonna give me a loan? I haven't got a job

BILLIE. One of those payday things, even?

TOBES. I haven't got a payday

BILLIE. Then sell some stuff

TOBES. Such as?

BILLIE. I don't know

TOBES. I haven't got anything!

BILLIE. Alright, I'm just trying to help

TOBES. You're trying to kick me out

BILLIE. I'm not

TOBES. You are

BILLIE. I'm just trying to treat you like a normal person

TOBES. I am a normal person

BILLIE. You know what I mean

TOBES. I don't know if I do

BILLIE. I'm just trying to carry on like before

TOBES. It's not like before, though, is it? Nothing's like before

BILLIE. Well that's life, isn't it? I'm sorry, Tobes, but that's what life is: one thing after another, that's how it goes. And I know it's all horrible, big, life-changing stuff for you and I'm sorry, I honestly am, but time hasn't stopped since you found your lump. So yeah, I know you don't want to have to deal with this as well, but you've got to find the money, Tobes, or go

TOBES. Go where?

BILLIE. That's up to you. You know where I think you should go, but

TOBES. I can't

BILLIE. You can

TOBES. She wants something else. Someone spontaneous or something

BILLIE. So be spontaneous. Call her. Go round, tell her how you feel

TOBES. I can't. Not now

BILLIE. Especially now. Why not? Use this thing to your advantage, Tobes. Tell her. Whatever it takes. To make yourself happy, I mean. Or what's the point in anything?

TOBES....

BILLIE. Look who knows what's around the corner? They might call you tomorrow and, god forbid, / but

TOBES. They've already called me

BILLIE. What?

TOBES. They've already called me

BILLIE. Since. But you've only just

TOBES. Yeah. I know. Can't be good, can it?

BILLIE. What do you mean it can't be good? What did they say, Tobes?

TOBES....

BILLIE. Tobes

TOBES. I don't know

BILLIE. You don't know?

TOBES. I didn't answer

BILLIE. Why not? You didn't answer, why didn't you answer, Tobes?

TOBES. I don't know! I don't know, I don't know, Billie, I don't, I just, it rang and I took it out of my pocket and I stood there and I looked at it like it was some kind of bomb, like it was a landmine I'd just stepped on and I couldn't move or I'd set it off, and I don't know why. I don't. I mean it doesn't make any sense, does it? It's happened. It's already happened if I answer the phone or not. If my insides are eating me up, then I mean, I'm already dead, or the chemo's booked, or the whatever, it's

in the diary, it's, it's happening. Time is happening, you're
right. So what am I waiting for? Pick up the phone. I mean.
Do it, you know? Do it! Pick up! But I don't, I just stand there,
in the street staring at it. After all of. Everything. I'm still
doing that. I mean. What is wrong with me?

BILLIE....

TOBES. What's wrong with me, Bill?

BILLIE. I don't know, mate. But someone does. So let's call
them back and find out, shall we?

Thirteen

A communal stairwell.

TOBES *and* JERMAINE.

JERMAINE. Hello, mate

TOBES. You have got to be kidding me

JERMAINE. Jermaine

TOBES. I know who you are. Are you living here now?

JERMAINE. No

TOBES. Have you moved in?

JERMAINE. I just told you

TOBES. But you are together? You and Beth? You're a couple?

JERMAINE. Look, mate

TOBES. I'm not your mate

JERMAINE. I know what you're thinking, but we didn't cross
over, me and you. She's a good girl

TOBES. Oh

JERMAINE. You alright?

TOBES. No, I feel sick

JERMAINE. You want a glass of water?

TOBES. What? No. I don't

JERMAINE. Alright

TOBES. Is she in? Where is she?

JERMAINE. No, she's out

TOBES. Out where?

JERMAINE. I can't remember

TOBES. When's she back?

JERMAINE. I dunno. Late though

TOBES. You don't know where she's gone, you said

JERMAINE. I don't. But I know she's back late. Can I take a message?

TOBES. Just tell her to call me

JERMAINE. No, I don't think so

TOBES. What?

JERMAINE. I don't think I'm gonna do that

TOBES. Why not?

JERMAINE. If she wanted to call you, she'd call you. So

TOBES. Just tell her to answer her phone then, please?

JERMAINE. No, mate. Same thing: if she wanted to do it

TOBES. Just tell her

JERMAINE. Look I don't want to be difficult

TOBES. Then tell her

JERMAINE. She obviously doesn't want to talk to you, / so

TOBES. Did she say that?

JERMAINE. If she's not answering her phone

TOBES. Did she tell you that?

JERMAINE. I think it's pretty / clear   .

TOBES. Did she tell you that she doesn't want to talk to me?

JERMAINE. Yeah

TOBES. I don't believe you

JERMAINE. Well that's up to you

TOBES. I need to talk to her

JERMAINE. The problem is she doesn't need to talk to you, so

TOBES. I need to tell her something. She's gonna want to hear it

JERMAINE. Is it about your operation? Cos she already knows about that, mate

TOBES. What?

JERMAINE. Everyone knows, don't they? It's common knowledge.

TOBES....

JERMAINE. And look. For what it's worth

TOBES. Don't

JERMAINE. No, I'm saying

TOBES. Don't

JERMAINE. I'm only saying

TOBES. Don't say you feel sorry for me, / or

JERMAINE. But I do

TOBES. Don't say it or I might have to go and jump off the roof

JERMAINE. Look, mate

TOBES. I'm not your mate!

JERMAINE. Alright. I don't want a row

TOBES. Then tell her to pick up her phone

JERMAINE. I've said what I'm gonna say

TOBES. You've told her not to

JERMAINE. What?

TOBES. You've told her / not to

JERMAINE. Why would I do that?

TOBES. I dunno. You're threatened

JERMAINE. By you? The Womble?

TOBES. …

JERMAINE. Don't be stupid

TOBES. What did you just say?

JERMAINE. That's what they're calling you, mate

TOBES. Who is?

JERMAINE. People

TOBES. What people? Beth?

JERMAINE. Just people

TOBES. Is Beth making jokes about me?

JERMAINE. What difference does it make? You're history, mate

TOBES. Yeah, I am. I'm dying. Mate. I'll let you tell her, shall I?

JERMAINE. What?

TOBES. I'm riddled

JERMAINE. Are you serious?

TOBES. …

JERMAINE. Come in. Come on, come in, I'll go and get her

TOBES. You'll go and. Is she in there?

JERMAINE. Yeah. She told me to get rid of you, / but

TOBES. Tell me you're joking

JERMAINE. What sort of a joke would that be?

TOBES. Oh what a

JERMAINE. Careful

TOBES. What a, what / a

JERMAINE. I mean it. Watch your mouth

TOBES. Or what? I mean what are you going to do? I'm already dead

JERMAINE. Look

TOBES. No, you look. I want you to do me a favour

JERMAINE. No

TOBES. I think you will

JERMAINE. You wanna bet?

TOBES. Call it a dying request. Tell her

JERMAINE. Steady

TOBES. I want a single orchid on the coffin.

Fourteen

A hallway.

TOBES *and* LIZA.

LIZA. Tobes

TOBES. Sorry / I know

LIZA. What for?

TOBES. I know it's late

LIZA. That's fine

TOBES. Again

LIZA. No it's fine

TOBES. No I know, I know it's not, it's late and you just want to be asleep and, and growing your bump / and

LIZA. I'm just watching *Newsnight*

TOBES. I really, really need to speak to Joff, that's all

LIZA. He's not here

TOBES. He's

LIZA. He's away

TOBES. Away where?

LIZA. For the weekend. A stag do out in the sticks / somewhere

TOBES. Whose?

LIZA. Jason, from his work

TOBES. Jason? How's he getting married?

LIZA. She's horrible, apparently

TOBES. Still

LIZA. Try his mobile?

TOBES. It's going straight to answerphone

LIZA. What do you need him for?

TOBES. ...

LIZA. What is it, Tobes? What's wrong?

TOBES. ...

LIZA. You haven't had your results, have you?

TOBES. ...

LIZA. Have you had your results, Tobes?

TOBES. Yeah

LIZA. And?

   Beat.

TOBES. It was just a cyst, Liza

   Beat.

LIZA. A what?

TOBES. A hydrocele, yeah

LIZA. You had a cyst?

TOBES. And they took away my

LIZA. Jesus, Tobes

TOBES. I know

LIZA. So that's it?

TOBES. They took away, I could sue, I think. Do you think
I should?

LIZA. Sue who?

TOBES. The hospital

LIZA. What for?

TOBES. For negligence, or

LIZA. No, I mean: what for? Why?

TOBES. Why? They got it wrong

LIZA. Well no well maybe, but they / did

TOBES. Maybe?

LIZA. They did what they thought was best. It was a precaution

TOBES. No, a precaution is supposed to stop something
bad from happening and this is, I mean this is about as
bad as it gets

LIZA. But you're in the clear

TOBES. What's, what's, what's clear about it?

LIZA. You won't have to go / through

TOBES. What's clear about anything now?

LIZA. You won't have to face chemotherapy, / or

TOBES. But if I did, just if I did, I'd have something, wouldn't
I? I'd have a reason to feel like this

LIZA. Like what?

TOBES. Like this. I mean look at me. I'm on my knees. I'm
broken. I'm drowning. And every time I turn around there's

someone else who just seems to be doing it. Living. Swimming. Properly. Easily. And I don't know how. I don't understand it. I mean look at you, Jesus, you've got a flat, you've got a decent job, six months from now you'll have a kid

LIZA. Well, hopefully

TOBES. You'll have made a whole new life. All I've ever made is beans on toast. Seriously. If I dropped down dead tomorrow, what would people actually say? He liked football. He got a B in A-level Maths. And History. He had a girlfriend we all fell in love with once, but then he didn't again

LIZA. Have you thought about talking to someone, Tobes?

TOBES. I'm talking to you

LIZA. You know what I mean. A counsellor. Or a group maybe

TOBES. I'm not mad, Liza

LIZA. I'm not saying you are

TOBES. I'm just.

Beat.

He can't say it.

So she says it for him.

LIZA. Sad

TOBES. Yeah.

The reality of that hits him.

Yeah.

LIZA....

TOBES. I am.

LIZA....

TOBES. I'm really

LIZA....

TOBES. I'm really, really

Beat.

It's tough to watch by now.

LIZA. That's alright

TOBES. It's not

LIZA. You're allowed to be. For a while, Tobes. But this is the end of it now, isn't it? It's over. It's good news. Great news, in fact. So let this be a line in the sand, eh? Whatever happens, from here-on-out, there'll always be before and after this, won't there? And the before wasn't going that well, so let it go. Put it behind you. Start again. From here. From something good.

Beat.

TOBES. I told Beth I was dying

LIZA. Really?

TOBES. Yeah. Well, no. I told her boyfriend I was dying. I think he lives there now

LIZA. Blimey.

TOBES....

LIZA. That is pretty dark, Tobes

TOBES. Yeah

LIZA. You might have to tell her you're not at some point

TOBES. Yeah. I will

LIZA. Or you could just go back round there in six months' time and pretend to haunt her?

They smile.

Beat.

TOBES. I'm sorry. For

LIZA. Don't be

TOBES. I am though

LIZA. Don't be. Stop it. Move on. Good things.

Beat.

TOBES. You're gonna be a really good mum

LIZA. Well let's hope so. Joff's its dad, so.

They smile again.

Good things. Good things good things good things good things.

Fifteen

A community-centre hall.

TOBES *and* JAMIE.

JAMIE. You're early

TOBES. Am I? I thought

JAMIE. Doesn't start till half-eight

TOBES. Okay. I thought it was eight / for

JAMIE. Half-past

TOBES. Okay

JAMIE. You can wait in here though, if you want

TOBES. Right. Thanks

JAMIE. S'alright

TOBES. Are you the leader, or

JAMIE. The leader?

TOBES. Of the thing

JAMIE. The pack?

TOBES. The

JAMIE. The leader of the pack?

TOBES. The group

JAMIE. Me? No. There's not really a leader anyway. Well there is; there's a bloke called Jonathan who brings the drums and that with him, but it's a bit of a free-for-all, really

TOBES. The drums?

JAMIE. Yeah there's always a bit of that first: sitting about in a circle hitting something for a while. Don't ask me why. To make an atmosphere or something. But then we just go round and. Whatever, really. Some people don't talk, some do. It's up to you

TOBES. Okay. Alright. Well that sounds

JAMIE. About as much fun as waterboarding, yeah. It's alright. I mainly come for the pub after; there's a couple of the lads are alright.

TOBES....

JAMIE. I'm Jamie

TOBES. Tobes

JAMIE. Tobes?

TOBES. Yeah

JAMIE. Tobes

TOBES. Tobes.

Beat.

JAMIE. Alright. You want a coffee, Tobes? There's a machine out there. While you wait

TOBES. Oh

JAMIE. Nescafé, / but.

TOBES. No I don't really drink coffee

JAMIE. Good for you, tastes like hot death

TOBES. But you still drink it?

JAMIE. Like a fish

TOBES. Why? If you don't like the taste

JAMIE. Same reason I smoke, I suppose

TOBES. Why's that?

JAMIE. No idea. Why does anyone do anything?

They smile.

You come a long way, Tobes?

TOBES. Um. Well. I mean

JAMIE. I'm asking where you live, not / like

TOBES. Oh. Yeah, no. Sorry. Not far, I've actually moved back home for a bit. Just round the corner. So. You?

JAMIE. You know the hospice at the top of the hill?

TOBES....

JAMIE. There's a block of flats just behind that

TOBES. Jesus, I thought you meant

JAMIE. I'm joking. I'm in the hospice.

TOBES....

JAMIE. Yeah it's always a bit of a conversation-killer. It's not as bad as it sounds. It's a bit like being back at uni, just with more pensioners. People come and visit and that. My ex brings my little boy up once a week

TOBES. You've got a son?

JAMIE. Joshy. Not so little now. School soon, the poor bugger. He's got this birthmark on his face. They're gonna crucify him when he's older

TOBES. Is it bad?

JAMIE. Bad enough. He's a looker otherwise, takes after his mum. But you know what kids are like

TOBES. Cruel

JAMIE. Cruel. Unbelievably cruel. That's life though, eh?

TOBES. Yeah

JAMIE. What

TOBES. No, just. I know the feeling

JAMIE. Yeah?

TOBES. This last month-or-so

JAMIE. Tell me about it.

TOBES. ...

JAMIE. I mean tell me about it

TOBES. Oh

JAMIE. Only if you want / to

TOBES. No, yeah, my girlfriend left me for her personal trainer

JAMIE. Right. I meant tell me about your

TOBES. Sorry. Yeah. I had a lump and

JAMIE. How long for?

TOBES. I mean quite a while, but

JAMIE. Six months?

TOBES. Er. No. Two years. Give or take

JAMIE *laughs/smiles*.

Why's that

JAMIE. I thought I was bad. I left it eighteen months for mine

TOBES. Yeah?

JAMIE. Yeah. What a pair of

TOBES. Yeah, what pair / of

JAMIE. So what happened?

TOBES. I had it. Removed

JAMIE. Just the one?

TOBES. Yeah

JAMIE. Which?

TOBES. The left

JAMIE. So you're alright, then?

TOBES. ...

JAMIE. Get it? All right?

TOBES. Oh, yeah

JAMIE. You'll hear loads of that here

TOBES. The thing I was.

JAMIE. ...

TOBES. Alright. I mean. It was just a cyst

JAMIE. You what?

TOBES. Yeah I know

JAMIE. So there's nothing wrong with you?

TOBES. Well I mean, no there's plenty wrong with me but

JAMIE. Such as?

Beat.

TOBES. Well I didn't get the implant, for a start, so.

JAMIE. ...

TOBES. I just. I feel a bit.

JAMIE. ...

TOBES. Did you get one?

JAMIE. Me?

TOBES. Yeah

JAMIE. No

TOBES. No?

JAMIE. They hollowed me out, Tobes.

TOBES. ...

JAMIE. I'm like a Halloween pumpkin down there

TOBES. Right

JAMIE. Yeah. I look like your dog after he's been to the vet's.

TOBES....

JAMIE. But they just scooped yours out, did they?

TOBES....

JAMIE. Lucky boy

TOBES. But I'm not. Not really, I mean. I'd have been better off a hundred years ago, wouldn't I? They just wouldn't have had this operation. And a hundred years into the future they probably wouldn't have done it either. They'd have told me it was fine. But we live in the middle. So as it is

JAMIE. As it is you'll live to a ripe old age with one side of your nut-sack hanging lower. That's it. Poor you. And as it is I'll die this side of Christmas. When they've finally finished turning me inside out. And as it is my little boy will come home from school one day when he's seven or eight crying his eyes out and asking why everyone's mean to him because of the wine stain on his face and I won't be there to pick him up and rub his back and tell him they can all go and hang themselves for all we care cos he'll grow up to be the better person. So you're right: as it is, the science is a monumental disappointment, but not to you, cos you can go and live your life now, can't you? You can climb a mountain. Run yourself a marathon. Sit on a beach and watch the sun rise till you're old and grey. But if you'd rather mope and cry and whinge then you can go and do it to someone else, cos I'm not having you round here moaning to me cos you're too proud to have a plastic bollock.

Sixteen

A beach somewhere.

TOBES *watches the sun come up.*

After a while, IZZY *enters.*

TOBES. Izzy.

IZZY....

TOBES. Tobes. We met in the bar the other night

IZZY. Tobes

TOBES. At the hotel

IZZY. Yeah, yeah, no

TOBES. We had a drink

IZZY. I remember

TOBES. You were laughing at the karaoke

IZZY. Yes. I was

TOBES. And then you went and did it

IZZY. And you didn't. I remember it well, / yeah

TOBES. Sorry, I can't sing, that's all

IZZY. Did you hear me up there?

TOBES. You were good. And the girl with you

IZZY. Libby

TOBES. She was great

IZZY. She was good, I was energetic

TOBES. I mean. Yeah, you were definitely energetic.

   They smile.

   Big night?

IZZY. Er. Yeah. I suppose

TOBES. I mean it must have been, it's half-past five

IZZY. Is it? No wonder I feel like this

TOBES. Where's Libby?

IZZY. Oh she met someone, so

TOBES. Right

IZZY. One of the locals actually. Slightly terrifying. But. She took him back, so. You?

TOBES. Me?

IZZY. What are you doing here? At

TOBES. Oh I couldn't sleep, that's all. Thought I'd watch the sun come up for a bit

IZZY. How very poetic of you

TOBES. No, I just. I sort of owe to someone, so

IZZY. You owe it to someone?

TOBES. It's. Yeah it's a bit of a long story

IZZY. Okay. Well. It's past my bedtime. So

TOBES. Listen, sorry, no, look, before you go, can I just. I want to apologise

IZZY. Apologise? What for?

TOBES. I sort of. Lied to you. The other night

IZZY. You lied to me?

TOBES. Yeah

IZZY. When?

TOBES. When I said I was here with my girlfriend. I'm not, I'm.

IZZY. …

TOBES. I'm with my mum

IZZY. You came on holiday with your mum?

TOBES. I know it's a bit. But I'd paid for the flights already and she needed a break / so

IZZY. So when you told me you had to get back to your girlfriend

TOBES. Yeah. I was lying, yeah

IZZY. Then. What? Then keep lying! Don't tell me now! That was fine! 'He's got a girlfriend, it's fine, you haven't just been completely rejected, it's cos he's got a girlfriend up in his room, otherwise he would've definitely said yes to a drink or a eighties duet or whatever'

TOBES. I would have

IZZY. But you didn't

TOBES. No I know, / but

IZZY. And you don't have a girlfriend. So. You just didn't fancy me

TOBES. I did

IZZY. Which is fine, by the way, but why tell me now?

TOBES. Honestly. I do. I do fancy you. I think you're. Yeah. I was kicking myself. Really. I was. Just before, even. When you got here just now. I was thinking about you. And then there you were. I promise you. For a minute I thought I'd made you up

IZZY. You what?

TOBES. I thought I'd imagined you, / or

IZZY. My god, what sort of a line is that?

TOBES. Honestly, I'm not. That's just. I'm a bit delirious, I haven't slept and, and. The point is: I think you're lovely. And. I'm sorry. I'm sorry I pretended I had a girlfriend when I don't

IZZY. So why did you?

TOBES. I've. I've only got one ball.

Beat.

IZZY. What?

TOBES. I've, yeah

IZZY. Like Hitler?

TOBES. No

IZZY. I'm not saying you're like Hitler

TOBES. I'm not

IZZY. No. Good

TOBES. But that's, that's why. I just, I didn't want to get to that bit, and

IZZY. Bit presumptuous

TOBES. No, I mean. Not just the other night, but, ever, really

IZZY. I'm kidding

TOBES. Okay

IZZY. So it's pretty recent, then?

TOBES. Well, yeah

IZZY. What happened? You catch it on a fence or something?

TOBES. Something like that

IZZY. And you haven't. Since. You haven't

TOBES. No. So that's why

IZZY. Well that's. Brilliant

TOBES. Is it?

IZZY. It's not brilliant. But

TOBES. No

IZZY. But

TOBES....

IZZY. When I was younger I had a boyfriend who only had pubes on the left-hand side. He'd spilt boiling water down himself when he was a kid, then had a skin graft from somewhere so he couldn't grow hair on the right. It was just. Shiny and. Yeah. I think that was probably weirder

TOBES. But you admit it's weird, then. Mine

IZZY. Well probably, yeah. But no one cares about the balls, do they? Not really. They're just the backing singers. So long as the frontman's doing his job

TOBES. Does your mother know what comes out of your mouth?

IZZY. I think she'd be more worried about some of the things that go into it.

They smile.

Look I should get back. Make sure Libby hasn't been cut up into a thousand pieces by her Spanish lover

TOBES. Jesus

IZZY. Sorry, yeah, I don't know why I said that. She's probably fine

TOBES. I hope so now

IZZY. So do I. Imagine

TOBES. No!

IZZY. Don't imagine, no, shut up, stop talking now. You think you've got issues.

They smile again.

TOBES. What are you doing tomorrow? Today, I mean. Later

IZZY. Er

TOBES. Do you want to climb a mountain?

IZZY. Sorry, what?

TOBES. I mean I think it's mainly walking really, but

IZZY. You're gonna climb a mountain?

TOBES. Yeah

IZZY. We are on very different holidays

TOBES. No it's just. I'm raising money for a thing

IZZY. Get you

TOBES. No, it's more of an apology than. It's complicated. The same long story. I'll tell you all about it on the way up

IZZY. I can't go and climb a mountain

TOBES. Why not?

IZZY. I've got these or flip-flops

TOBES. They can lend you something. The guides

IZZY. I can't climb up the stairs without feeling sick

TOBES. I'll carry you up on my back if I have to. Come.

IZZY....

TOBES. Please?

IZZY....

TOBES. Too much?

IZZY. No, no just quite. I dunno

TOBES. Why not? And then you never have to see me again.

IZZY....

TOBES. What else would you be doing?

Just then, JOEL *enters.*

JOEL. Sorry, I couldn't find anywhere without cameras

IZZY. Cameras?

JOEL. CCTV. I can't pee if I'm being watched. Hiya, sorry

TOBES. Hello

IZZY. This is Tobes

JOEL. Tobes. Nice name. Joel. Actually, no, don't shake that. Nice to meet you

TOBES. Yeah. You too

JOEL. You two are friends, are you?

TOBES. Er

IZZY. Yeah

JOEL. Lovely

TOBES. And you?

JOEL. Yeah we are now aren't we?

IZZY. Yeah

JOEL. Turns out we live close by back home as well. So no pressure, eh?

IZZY. What you think I'll just be turning up on your doorstep like that?

JOEL. Or like that:

He mimes a baby or a bump

'It's yours'

IZZY. You should be so lucky

JOEL. Hey you could do a lot worse yourself; I was under-sixteens county long-jump champion

IZZY. Were you?

JOEL. No, I came third, but

IZZY. Gutted

JOEL. I was. Still am a bit

TOBES. I'm still impressed

JOEL. Yeah? See, Tobes knows

IZZY. Well, lucky me

JOEL. Thank you. I'm glad you agree.

They smile.

IZZY. Look listen will you do me a favour and wait for me down by the thing on the corner? The statue thing? I'll catch you up

JOEL. Yeah?

IZZY. Yeah, I'll just be a minute

JOEL. Alright. Well, alright I'll see you later then, Tobes

TOBES. Yeah

JOEL. A bunch of us are going to watch the cup final this afternoon, actually, if you're up for it?

TOBES. The football?

JOEL. Izzy's coming, aren't you

TOBES. I'm. No I'm not really into football, so

JOEL. No?

TOBES. No, not really, no. Not any more anyway

JOEL. What, gone off it, have you?

TOBES. No, just. Trying to do other things

JOEL. Such as?

Beat.

TOBES. Yeah I'm not really sure yet.

Beat.

JOEL. Right. Well. The offer's there if you change your mind

TOBES. Thanks, yeah

JOEL. Alright. So I'll wait for you by the metal-fish thing

IZZY. Yeah. Two seconds. I'll catch you up

JOEL. Take it easy, Tobes

TOBES. Yeah I will. And you.

JOEL gives IZZY's hand a tiny squeeze as he passes and leaves.

He seems nice

IZZY. He sort of is, actually

TOBES. Good luck to him. To the both of you

IZZY. Holiday romances

TOBES. You never know. Stranger things have happened.

Beat.

IZZY. Thanks for the offer, Tobes. The walk

TOBES. Thank you. For the chat

IZZY. I'm sure I'll see you around

TOBES. No doubt. Unless I can get the ground to swallow me up first.

They smile.

IZZY. Don't be embarrassed

TOBES. No, I won't

IZZY. I meant about your

TOBES. Yeah. So did I

IZZY. Well. Good. I'll see you then

TOBES. Yeah

IZZY. You'll be alright if I leave you here, won't you? I mean you're not gonna go blind staring into the sun or something?

TOBES. No I'll. Yeah, I'll definitely

IZZY....

TOBES. I'll be all right.

They smile. Then IZZY *goes.*

Hold on TOBES.

End.

Other Titles in this Series

A Nick Hern Book

Growth first published in Great Britain in 2016 as a paperback original by Nick Hern Books Limited, The Glasshouse, 49a Goldhawk Road, London W12 8QP, in association with Paines Plough

Growth copyright © 2016 Luke Norris

Luke Norris has asserted his right to be identified as the author of this work

Cover image by Thread Design

Designed and typeset by Nick Hern Books, London
Printed in Great Britain by CPI Group (UK) Ltd

A CIP catalogue record for this book is available from the British Library

ISBN 978 1 84842 592 7